PIANO / VOCAL / GUITAR

budgetbooks

P9-BIY-812

JAZZ STANDARDS

ISBN 0-634-04063-4

HAL•LEONARD®
CORPORATION

7777 W. BLUEMOUND RD. P.O. BOX 13819 MILWAUKEE, WI 53213

Visit Hal Leonard Online at
www.halleonard.com

CONTENTS

ADIOS

English Words by EDDIE WOODS
Spanish Translation and Music by ENRIC MADRIGUERA

ALL OR NOTHING AT ALL

Words by JACK LAWRENCE
Music by ARTHUR ALTMAN

14

ALFIE
Theme from the Paramount Picture ALFIE

Words by HAL DAVID
Music by BURT BACHARACH

ALRIGHT, OKAY, YOU WIN

Words and Music by SID WYCHE
and MAYME WATTS

ALWAYS

Words and Music by
IRVING BERLIN

ALWAYS IN MY HEART
(Siempre En Mi Corazón)
from ALWAYS IN MY HEART

Music and Spanish Words by ERNESTO LECUONA
English Words by KIM GANNON

AQUELLOS OJOS VERDES
(Green Eyes)

Music by NILO MENENDEZ
Spanish Words by ADOLFO UTRERA
English Words by E. RIVERA and E. WOODS

AUTUMN IN NEW YORK

Words and Music by
VERNON DUKE

41

BÉSAME MUCHO
(Kiss Me Much)

Music and Spanish Words by CONSUELO VELAZQUEZ
English Words by SUNNY SKYLAR

BEWITCHED

from PAL JOEY

Words by LORENZ HART
Music by RICHARD RODGERS

Lyrics:

He's a fool and don't I know it. But a fool can have his charms.
Love's the same old sad sen-sa-tion. Late-ly I've not slept a wink.

I'm in love and don't I show it, like a babe in arms.
Since this half-pint im-i-ta-tion

put me on the blink. I'm wild a-gain, be-guiled a-gain, a

THE BLUE ROOM

from THE GIRL FRIEND

Words by LORENZ HART
Music by RICHARD RODGERS

BODY AND SOUL

Words by EDWARD HEYMAN,
ROBERT SOUR and FRANK EYTON
Music by JOHN GREEN

BLUE SKIES

from BETSY

Words and Music by
IRVING BERLIN

59

BRAZIL

Words and Music by S.K. RUSSELL
and ARY BARROSO

63

64

CALL ME IRRESPONSIBLE

from the Paramount Picture PAPA'S DELICATE CONDITION

Words by SAMMY CAHN
Music by JAMES VAN HEUSEN

CHEROKEE
(Indian Love Song)

Words and Music by
RAY NOBLE

CRY ME A RIVER

Words and Music by
ARTHUR HAMILTON

CLOSE AS PAGES IN A BOOK
from UP IN CENTRAL PARK

Words by DOROTHY FIELDS
Music by SIGMUND ROMBERG

DAY BY DAY

Theme from the Paramount Television Series DAY BY DAY

Words and Music by SAMMY CAHN,
AXEL STORDAHL and PAUL WESTON

83

84

DO NOTHIN'
TILL YOU HEAR FROM ME

Words and Music by DUKE ELLINGTON
and BOB RUSSELL

DAY DREAM

Words by JOHN LA TOUCHE
Music by DUKE ELLINGTON and BILLY STRAYHORN

DO YOU KNOW WHAT IT MEANS TO MISS NEW ORLEANS

Lyric by EDDIE DE LANGE
Music by LOUIS ALTER

FEVER

Words and Music by JOHN DAVENPORT
and EDDIE COOLEY

you all know.   Fe - ver is - n't   such a new thing,

E7   Am   5 Am

fe - ver start - ed long___ a - go.   burn.

Verse 3 Romeo loved Juliet
Juliet she felt the same,
When he put his arms around her, he said,
"Julie, baby you're my flame."

Chorus Thou givest fever, when we kisseth
Fever with my flaming youth,
Fever – I'm afire
Fever, yea I burn forsooth.

Verse 4 Captain Smith and Pocahantas
Had a very mad affair,
When her Daddy tried to kill him, she said,
"Daddy-o don't you dare."

Chorus Give me fever, with his kisses,
Fever when he holds me tight.
Fever – I'm his Missus
Oh Daddy won't you treat him right.

Verse 5 Now you've listened to my story
Here's the point that I have made:
Chicks were born to give you fever
Be it fahrenheit or centigrade.

Chorus They give you fever when you kiss them,
Fever if you live and learn.
Fever – till you sizzle
What a lovely way to burn.

DREAMY

Music by ERROLL GARNER
Lyric by SYDNEY SHAW

EARLY AUTUMN

Words by JOHNNY MERCER
Music by RALPH BURNS and WOODY HERMAN

Slowly, with feeling

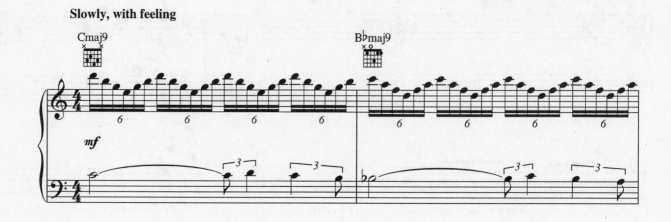

FLY ME TO THE MOON
(In Other Words)
featured in the Motion Picture ONCE AROUND

Words and Music by
BART HOWARD

Fm7 Ab/Bb D7-9
1 Gm7-5 C9 Cmaj7
oth - er words, please be true! In
Fm7 Ab/Bb Bb9 Eb(add9)
oth - er words, I love you.
2 Gm7-5 C7(#9) Fm7 Ab/Bb
true! In oth - er words,
Bb9 Bb7-9 Eb6
Guitar Tacet
I love you!
8va

FRENESÍ

Words and Music by
ALBERTO DOMINGUEZ

GEORGIA ON MY MIND

Words by STUART GORRELL
Music by HOAGY CARMICHAEL

Additional Lyric for Verse

Melodies bring memories that linger in my heart.
Make me think of Georgia;
Why did we ever part?
Some sweet day when blossoms fall and all the world's a song,
I'll go back to Georgia,
'cause that's where I belong.

THE GLORY OF LOVE

Words and Music by
BILLY HILL

122

when the world is through with us, we've got each oth - er's

arms. _____ You've got to win a lit - tle, lose a lit - tle,

and al-ways have the blues a lit - tle. That's the sto-ry of, that's the glo-ry of

love. _____ You've got to love. _____

GOOD MORNING HEARTACHE

Words and Music by DAN FISHER,
IRENE HIGGINBOTHAM and ERVIN DRAKE

Slow Blues tempo

GOD BLESS' THE CHILD

Words and Music by ARTHUR HERZOG JR.
and BILLIE HOLIDAY

HARLEM NOCTURNE

Words by DICK ROGERS
Music by EARLE HAGEN

134

HOW DEEP IS THE OCEAN
(How High Is the Sky)

Words and Music by
IRVING BERLIN

I CAN'T GET STARTED WITH YOU

from ZIEGFELD FOLLIES

Words by IRA GERSHWIN
Music by VERNON DUKE

I HEAR MUSIC

from the Paramount Picture DANCING ON A DIME

Words by FRANK LOESSER
Music by BURTON LANE

I COULD WRITE A BOOK

from PAL JOEY

Words by LORENZ HART
Music by RICHARD RODGERS

149

I DIDN'T KNOW WHAT TIME IT WAS

from TOO MANY GIRLS

Words by LORENZ HART
Music by RICHARD RODGERS

I GOT IT BAD AND THAT AIN'T GOOD

Words by PAUL FRANCIS WEBSTER
Music by DUKE ELLINGTON

158

159

I LET A SONG GO OUT OF MY HEART

Words and Music by DUKE ELLINGTON,
HENRY NEMO, JOHN REDMOND and IRVING MILLS

I WISH I WERE IN LOVE AGAIN

from BABES IN ARMS

Words by LORENZ HART
Music by RICHARD RODGERS

I'LL BE SEEING YOU

from RIGHT THIS WAY

Lyric by IRVING KAHAL
Music by SAMMY FAIN

Ca - the-dral bells were toll - ing _____ And our hearts sang on,

___ Was it the spell of Par - is _____ Or the A - pril dawn? _____

Who knows, _____ if we shall meet a - gain?

I'M BEGINNING TO SEE THE LIGHT

Words and Music by DON GEORGE, JOHNNY HODGES,
DUKE ELLINGTON and HARRY JAMES

Lyrics:

I nev-er cared much for moon-lit skies, I nev-er wink back at fire-flies, but now that the stars are in your eyes, I'm be-gin-ning to see the light. I

Then you came and caused a spark __ that's a four a-larm fire __ now. __

__ I nev-er made love by lan-tern shine, __ I

nev-er saw rain-bows in my wine, __ but now that your lips are

burn-ing mine, __ I'm be-gin-ning to see the light. __ I __

8vb

ISN'T IT ROMANTIC?

from the Paramount Picture LOVE ME TONIGHT

Words by LORENZ HART
Music by RICHARD RODGERS

I'M GONNA SIT RIGHT DOWN AND WRITE MYSELF A LETTER

from AIN'T MISBEHAVIN'

Lyric by JOE YOUNG
Music by FRED E. AHLERT

ILL WIND
(You're Blowin' Me No Good)
from COTTON CLUB PARADE

Lyric by TED KOEHLER
Music by HAROLD ARLEN

IN THE MOOD

By JOE GARLAND

IT COULD HAPPEN TO YOU

from the Paramount Picture AND THE ANGELS SING

Words by JOHNNY BURKE
Music by JAMES VAN HEUSEN

IT DON'T MEAN A THING
(If It Ain't Got That Swing)
from SOPHISTICATED LADIES

Words and Music by DUKE ELLINGTON
and IRVING MILLS

IT MIGHT AS WELL BE SPRING

from STATE FAIR

Lyrics by OSCAR HAMMERSTEIN II
Music by RICHARD RODGERS

IT NEVER ENTERED MY MIND

from HIGHER AND HIGHER

Words by LORENZ HART
Music by RICHARD RODGERS

I don't care if there's pow-der on my nose, I don't care if my hair-do is in place. I've lost the ver-y mean-ing of re-pose, I nev-er put a mud pack on my face. Oh, who'd have thought that I'd

IT'S EASY TO REMEMBER

from the Paramount Picture MISSISSIPPI

Words by LORENZ HART
Music by RICHARD RODGERS

209

210

JUST ONE MORE CHANCE

Words by SAM COSLOW
Music by ARTHUR JOHNSTON

215

THE LADY IS A TRAMP
from BABES IN ARMS

Words by LORENZ HART
Music by RICHARD RODGERS

THE LADY'S IN LOVE WITH YOU
from the Paramount Picture SOME LIKE IT HOT

Words by FRANK LOESSER
Music by BURTON LANE

Long be-fore the first kiss___ have you ev - er seen this?___

Refrain

If there's a gleam in her eye___ each time she straight-ens your tie,___

___ you'll know the la - dy's in love___ with you. If she can

dress for a date___ with - out that wait-ing you hate___ it means the la - dy's in love___

222

LAZY RIVER

from THE BEST YEARS OF OUR LIVES

Words and Music by HOAGY CARMICHAEL
and SIDNEY ARODIN

LAZY AFTERNOON
from THE GOLDEN APPLE

Words and Music by JOHN LATOUCHE
and JEROME MOROSS

LAZYBONES

Words and Music by HOAGY CARMICHAEL
and JOHNNY MERCER

Slow Blues

Long as there is chick-en gra-vy

on your rice, ___ ev-'ry-thing is nice.

LOVER
from the Paramount Picture LOVE ME TONIGHT

Words by LORENZ HART
Music by RICHARD RODGERS

236

238

LITTLE GIRL BLUE
from JUMBO

Words by LORENZ HART
Music by RICHARD RODGERS

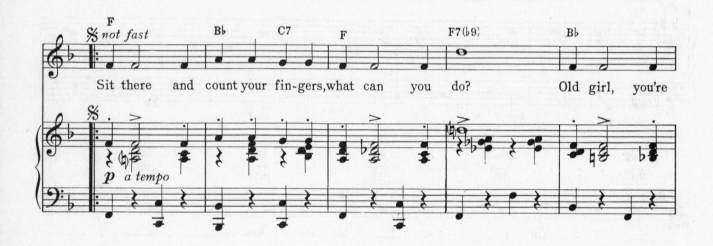

Sit there and count your fin-gers, what can you do? Old girl, you're

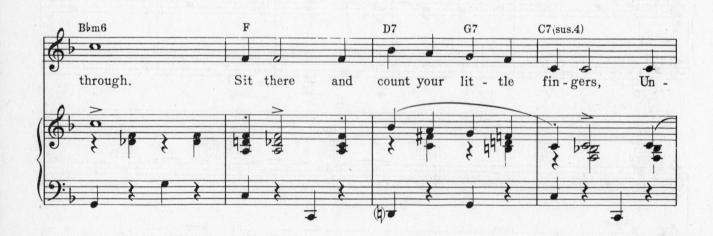

through. Sit there and count your lit-tle fin-gers, Un-

LOVE IS JUST AROUND THE CORNER

from the Paramount Picture HERE IS MY HEART

Words and Music by LEO ROBIN
and LEWIS E. GENSLER

LULLABY OF BIRDLAND

Words by GEORGE DAVID WEISS
Music by GEORGE SHEARING

MANHATTAN

from the Broadway Musical THE GARRICK GAIETIES

Words by LORENZ HART
Music by RICHARD RODGERS

We'll set - tle down right here in town.

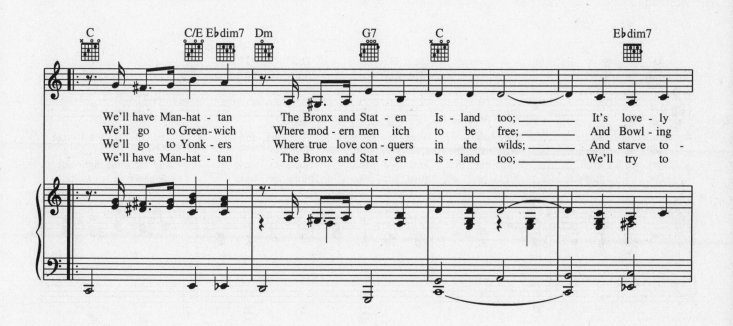

We'll have Man-hat - tan The Bronx and Stat - en Is - land too; _____ It's love - ly
We'll go to Green-wich Where mod - ern men itch to be free; _____ And Bowl - ing
We'll go to Yonk - ers Where true love con - quers in the wilds; _____ And starve to -
We'll have Man-hat - tan The Bronx and Stat - en Is - land too; _____ We'll try to

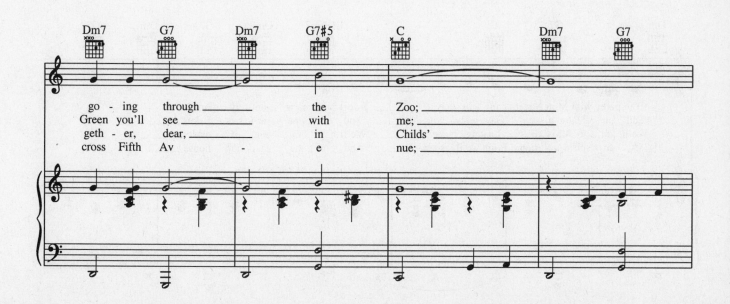

go - ing through _____ the Zoo; _____
Green you'll see _____ with me; _____
geth - er, dear, _____ in Childs' _____
cross Fifth Av - e - nue; _____

MIDNIGHT SUN

Words and Music by LIONEL HAMPTON,
SONNY BURKE and JOHNNY MERCER

Slowly, with a beat

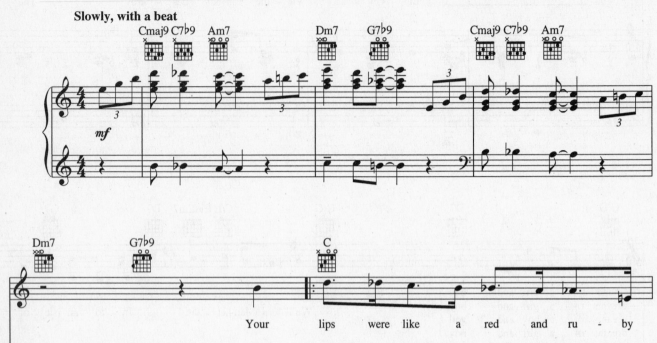

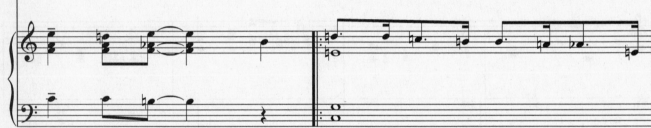

Your lips were like a red and ru - by

chal - ice, warm - er than the sum - mer night,

261

MONA LISA
from the Paramount Picture CAPTAIN CAREY, U.S.A.

Words and Music by JAY LIVINGSTON
and RAY EVANS

MY FAVORITE THINGS
from THE SOUND OF MUSIC

Lyrics by OSCAR HAMMERSTEIN II
Music by RICHARD RODGERS

MY FOOLISH HEART
from MY FOOLISH HEART

Words by NED WASHINGTON
Music by VICTOR YOUNG

Slowly and expressively

MY HEART STOOD STILL

from A CONNECTICUT YANKEE

Words by LORENZ HART
Music by RICHARD RODGERS

273

MY ROMANCE
from JUMBO

Words by LORENZ HART
Music by RICHARD RODGERS

MY SHIP

from the Musical Production LADY IN THE DARK

Words by IRA GERSHWIN
Music by KURT WEILL

THE NEARNESS OF YOU
from the Paramount Picture ROMANCE IN THE DARK

Words by NED WASHINGTON
Music by HOAGY CARMICHAEL

NEVER LET ME GO

from the Paramount Picture THE SCARLET HOUR

Words and Music by JAY LIVINGSTON
and RAY EVANS

290

A NIGHTINGALE SANG IN BERKELEY SQUARE

Lyric by ERIC MASCHWITZ
Music by MANNING SHERWIN

*Pronounced "Bar-kley"

293

PERFIDIA

Words and Music by
ALBERTO DOMINGUEZ

298

SEPTEMBER SONG
from the Musical Play KNICKERBOCKER HOLIDAY

Words by MAXWELL ANDERSON
Music by KURT WEILL

SKYLARK

Words by JOHNNY MERCER
Music by HOAGY CARMICHAEL

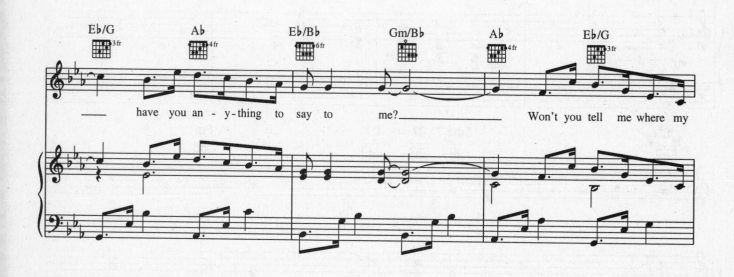

SPEAK LOW
from the Musical Production ONE TOUCH OF VENUS

Words by OGDEN NASH
Music by KURT WEILL

WALTZ FOR DEBBY

Lyric by GENE LEES
Music by BILL EVANS

STELLA BY STARLIGHT
from the Paramount Picture THE UNINVITED

Words by NED WASHINGTON
Music by VICTOR YOUNG

G6/9
and not a dream.
(Boy): My
(Girl): She's
C#m7♭5
2fr
F#7
Bm7♭5
heart and I a - gree
all of these and more
E7
Am7♭5
she's ev - 'ry - thing
she's ev - 'ry - thing
D7
G(add9)
on earth to me.
that you'd a - dore.

TANGERINE
from the Paramount Picture THE FLEET'S IN

Words by JOHNNY MERCER
Music by VICTOR SCHERTZINGER

THANKS FOR THE MEMORY

from the Paramount Picture BIG BROADCAST OF 1938

Words and Music by LEO ROBIN
and RALPH RAINGER

324

THAT OLD BLACK MAGIC

from the Paramount Picture STAR SPANGLED RHYTHM

Words by JOHNNY MERCER
Music by HAROLD ARLEN

329

TICO TICO
(Tico No Fuba)

Words and Music by ZEQUINHA ABREU,
ALOYSIO OLIVEIRA and ERVIN DRAKE

333

334

THE WAY YOU LOOK TONIGHT

from SWING TIME

Words by DOROTHY FIELDS
Music by JEROME KERN

338

YOU BROUGHT A NEW KIND OF LOVE TO ME

from the Paramount Picture THE BIG POND

Words and Music by SAMMY FAIN,
IRVING KAHAL and PIERRE NORMAN

WHAT KIND OF FOOL AM I?

from the Musical Production STOP THE WORLD—I WANT TO GET OFF

Words and Music by LESLIE BRICUSSE
and ANTHONY NEWLEY

Moderately slow

What kind of fool am I? Who nev-er fell in love,_____ It seems that

I'm the on-ly one that I have been think-ing of._____ What kind of

man is this?_____ An emp-ty shell,_____ A lone-ly cell in which an
(life)

WHEN SUNNY GETS BLUE

Lyric by JACK SEGAL
Music by MARVIN FISHER

YOU'RE NOBODY
'TIL SOMEBODY LOVES YOU

Words and Music by RUSS MORGAN,
LARRY STOCK and JAMES CAVANAUGH